Power Play

The Ultimate Guide to Mastering Political Influence and Winning Campaigns

Politics 101

Steven Scott

Contents

Introduction

Money, Law, and Politics: By mastering these three pillars, you will obtain real success and influence. In this guidebook, we zero in on politics.

Power Play is the essential manual for political incumbents, challengers, and campaign managers. It is the key to harnessing political influence by crafting messages that resonate deeply with the human spirit. Designed for incumbents striving to maintain their reign, challengers bold enough to shake the status quo, and campaign managers who skillfully navigate the treacherous waters of political warfare, this guidebook brims with unmatched intrigue and wisdom.

Drawing on my years of experience as a former campaign manager and political consultant, I have navigated the highs and lows of the political landscape, learning invaluable lessons from every setback and victory. With a steadfast commitment to practicality and effectiveness, Power Play offers a clear roadmap to success. Each page is loaded with actionable insights and strategic maneuvers, providing you with the tools to navigate the complex twists and turns of the political world with confidence and precision.

You will encounter the word "must" frequently throughout this guidebook - not as a suggestion, but as a mandate. Make no mistake: this is no casual stroll through the halls of power. To emerge victorious in the unforgiving arena of politics, you must have an unwavering "yes I can" attitude in addition to adopting the principles outlined within these pages.

Whether you're a battle-hardened veteran or a fresh-faced newcomer, Power Play is the quintessential guidebook for political incumbents, challengers, and campaign managers.

Part One

Mastering the Political Maze

Incumbents and challengers entangled in a quest for influence and legitimacy must know and understand how to unlock the gears of governance and unravel the strategies that shape their political destiny.

Chapter 1

Strategic Decision-Making
Navigating Complex Choices

IN THE GRAND theater of politics, decision-making is the spotlight that defines impactful leadership. The ability to make informed, rational choices is essential for anyone in power, as it establishes the course of public welfare. Mastering this process is key to capturing the hearts and minds of voters for political incumbents, challengers, and their campaign managers

Incumbents:

Incumbents, those currently holding positions of authority, have refined their decision-making process through the wealth of knowledge and experience gained during their time in office. Their approach is grounded in several key factors:

• **Experience**: Having navigated the complex landscape of governance, which involves making tough decisions, handling crises, and managing diverse issues, incumbents possess a deep understanding of the intricacies of political leadership.

• **Historical Insight**: Past performances serve as a compass for incumbents. The mistakes and successes of the past become crucial learning experiences, offering valuable lessons that help make better decisions in the future.

• **Data-Driven Insights**: Utilizing data and evidence-based research is a hallmark of incumbents' decision-making. This approach allows for more accurate and effective choices, minimizing reliance on intuition alone and ensuring decisions are backed by solid evidence.

• **Stakeholder Input**: Listening to the voices of various stakeholders, including citizens, colleagues, experts, and interest groups, is essential. Their input provides a broad perspective, helping incumbents make informed community concerns and need decisions.

Challengers:

Challengers, seeking to unseat incumbents, bring a different energy and approach to decision-making. Their process is characterized by:

• **Visionary Thinking**: Challengers are often seen as visionaries, architects of change who envision a brighter and more prosperous future. Their vision drives their actions and decisions, inspiring hope and possibility.

• **Innovative Approaches**: Unconstrained by the traditions and routines that incumbents may adhere to, challengers bring fresh perspectives and innovative solutions. Their ability to think outside the box enables them to propose bold ideas to address current problems, pushing the boundaries of conventional thinking.

• **Courage and Determination**: What sets challengers apart is their rebellious passion. They are unafraid to confront and disrupt the status quo, driven by a strong desire to make a meaningful impact. Their courage and determination are key in galvanizing support and driving change.

Campaign Managers:

Campaign managers play a crucial role in shaping the decision-making narratives of both incumbents and challengers. They must craft compelling stories that highlight the strengths and unique qualities of their candidates, ensuring these narratives resonate with voters.

• **For Incumbents**: Campaign managers should emphasize their candidate's wealth of experience, historical insight, data-driven decision-making, and ability to incorporate diverse stakeholder input. The narrative must paint a picture of steady, reliable leadership that has proven effective over time.

• **For Challengers**: Campaign managers need to highlight visionary thinking, innovative approaches, and the courage to challenge the status quo. The story must focus on the promise of a brighter future and the fresh, dynamic leadership the challenger brings.

Chapter 2

Championing Transparency
Building Trust and Credibility

TRANSPARENCY in political decision-making is a practical necessity for effective governance. Transparency is the bedrock upon which trust is built, ensuring that citizens have the information they need to hold their government accountable and participate meaningfully in the democratic process.

Incumbents:

Transparency is a powerful shield against the doubts and suspicions that can erode public trust. Incumbents have a unique opportunity to showcase their dedication to serving the public by openly sharing information and being clear about their actions and decisions. Embracing transparency serves as a testament to their integrity and encourages a deeper connection with constituents. This openness reinforces a steadfast commitment to the public's best interests and solidifies incumbents' roles as trustworthy guardians of truth.

Key Processes:

• **Regular Updates**: Hold frequent press conferences and release detailed reports on governmental activities.

• **Open Data**: Make governmental data easily accessible to the public.

• **Responsive Communication**: Engage with citizens through various platforms to address their concerns promptly.

• **Clear Documentation:** Provide thorough explanations for policy decisions and legislative actions.

Challengers:

Transparency is the most potent weapon in the political arena. It serves as a sword of truth, designed to cut through the concealed errors and hidden agendas of incumbents. The promise of open governance resonates with voters eager for change and honesty. By championing transparency, challengers demonstrate a commitment to better governance, free from secrecy and corruption. Utilizing transparency challengers clarify their vision for a brighter future convincing the public that they are the rightful custodians of trust.

Key Strategies:

• **Transparency Pledge:** Publicly commit to specific transparency measures, such as publishing financial records and meeting minutes.

• **Expose Secrecy**: Highlight instances where incumbents have failed to be transparent and contrast this with a vision of open governance.

• **Engage with the Public**: Use social media, town halls, and other forums to actively engage with voters and discuss transparency.

• **Policy Proposals**: Outline clear, actionable policies aimed at increasing governmental transparency.

Campaign Managers;

Architects of political strategy, campaign managers play a crucial role in weaving transparency into the fabric of their candidate's narrative. When supporting an incumbent they must highlight their track record of openness and accountability and for challengers they must emphasize their pledge to bring clarity and honesty to governance. Effective communication of these messages captures the attention and trust of voters, making transparency a central theme of the campaign.

Key Tactics:

• **Messaging**: Develop a clear and consistent message around the importance of transparency.

• **Storytelling**: Use real-life examples and stories to illustrate the benefits of transparency.

• **Media Engagement**: Ensure the campaign's transparency efforts are well-covered by the media.

• **Voter Education**: Educate voters on how transparency impacts their lives and why it is crucial for effective governance.

Chapter 3

Crafting Effective Policies

Transforming Ideas into Action

"Working policies" refers to a set of guidelines, principles, and plans that are actively implemented by those in power to govern and manage various aspects of society.

Incumbents:

As tacticians of societal evolution, executing strategic maneuvers designed to promote progress. They are the pillars of stability, ensuring continuous development and guiding us towards a prosperous future. Their actions are not arbitrary but carefully planned to adapt to the evolving needs and circumstances of our social structure.

Challengers:

Challengers stir the collective conscience of a society yearning for change. They tap into the deep-seated desire for transformation, awakening a shared sense of urgency and motivation among the people. Through impassioned advocacy and bold proposals, they confront existing norms, pushing the boundaries of conventional thinking. Presenting new ideas and solutions that promise improvement and progress.

Campaign Managers:

The masterminds behind the scenes must understand that effective storytelling is crucial in capturing attention and moving voters. By highlighting the achievements of incumbents and the innovative visions of challengers, campaign managers craft narratives that resonate with the public, shaping perceptions and driving political engagement.

Chapter 4

Anticipating Challenges
Staying Ahead of the Curve

EFFECTIVE LEADERSHIP INVOLVES NOT JUST REACTING to problems as they occur but also predicting potential issues and preparing for them in advance. Leaders have the responsibility to anticipate difficulties and obstacles that may arise in the future.

Incumbents:

As masters of strategy and guardians of public trust they use their influence to shape the trajectory of policy with unwavering resolve, courage and conviction. By leveraging their authority in difficult times their firm determination, bravery, and strong belief in their actions guide the public through adversity, ensuring the public's trust is not misplaced.

Challengers:

Through strategic maneuvering aimed to tip the scales of power, they employ clever tactics such as building coalitions, leveraging media, mobilizing public opinion, and seizing political opportunities to gain an advantage. They vigilantly monitor the actions and policies of incumbents, seeking weaknesses to exploit. Voicing dissent, they publicly express disagreement with current policies, highlighting issues and rallying support for their cause. Their goal is to identify cracks in the armor of the status quo and persuade others that change is necessary and possible.

Campaign Managers:

Campaign managers shape the political landscape by crafting compelling narratives that resonate with voters. By presenting a balanced view of leadership in action they highlight the strategic foresight of incumbents and the vigilant advocacy of challengers

Chapter 5

Understanding Political Ideologies
Mapping the Spectrum

THESE IDEOLOGIES PROVIDE frameworks for understanding and interpreting political issues that shape people's views on how societies should be organized and governed.

- **Capitalism**: an economic system where private individuals or businesses, rather than the government, own and control the means of production, such as factories, businesses, and resources. It encourages entrepreneurship, innovation, and the accumulation of wealth.
- **Liberalism**: emphasizes individual freedom, equality, and the protection of civil liberties. It advocates for limited government intervention in the economy, free markets, democratic governance, and the rule of law.
- **Conservatism**: prioritizes tradition, stability, and the preservation of existing social institutions and hierarchies. It advocates for limited government, free markets, individual responsibility, and a strong emphasis on family values and national identity.
- **Socialism**: seeks to address economic inequality and promote social justice by advocating for collective ownership

and democratic control of the means of production. It argues for redistributive policies, government intervention in the economy, and the provision of social welfare programs to ensure equitable outcomes for all members of society.

- **Communism**: aims to create a classless, stateless society where the means of production are owned collectively and goods and services are distributed based on need. It advocates for the eventual dissolution of the state and the establishment of a utopian society.

- **Fascism**: an authoritarian ideology characterized by extreme nationalism, militarism, and the suppression of dissent. It emphasizes the superiority of the nation or race, rejects liberal democracy, and advocates for a strong, centralized state led by a charismatic leader.

- **Anarchism**: rejects hierarchical forms of authority and advocates for the abolition of the state, capitalism, and other oppressive institutions. It envisions decentralized, self-governing communities based on voluntary cooperation and mutual aid.

Chapter 6

Navigating Power Dynamics

Leveraging Influence for Success

THE ABILITY TO influence or control the behavior, decisions, and outcomes of others, is the function of relationship leveraging which individuals or groups utilize to negotiate power.

Power Brokers:

Power is not a static entity but a dynamic force expressed through various means, such as persuasion, coercion, negotiation, and collaboration. Understanding where power originates is essential for illuminating the key issues that take center stage in politics. Power can stem from institutional authority, popular support, economic influence, or social networks. Recognizing these sources provides insight into the motivations and interests driving political actors and agendas. These individuals or groups possess the ability to shape political discourse and decision-making by exploiting their relationships and interactions.

Incumbents:

As seasoned leaders, incumbents understand that their power is derived from both their authority and their ability to inspire trust and cooperation among the public and other political actors. Their leadership is defined by their ability to harness the power dynamics at play and use them to steer the public towards progress and stability. They must navigate a complex web of relationships and interactions to maintain their influence and achieve their policy goals. By applying their influence strategically, incumbents shape the trajectory of policy and address major concerns with unwavering resolve.

Challengers:

Through strategic maneuvering and vocal dissent, challengers aim to shift the power dynamics in their favor, advocating for change and highlighting alternative solutions enabling them to rally support and challenge the status quo. They scrutinize the origins of incumbents' power, identifying weaknesses and vulnerabilities to exploit. Their effectiveness lies in their capacity to mobilize public opinion, build coalitions, and influence media to tip the scales of power.

Campaign Managers:

In the political arena effective storytelling captures attention and ideas move voters. Whether highlighting the strategic mastery of incumbents or the disruptive potential of challengers, campaign managers play a pivotal role in shaping the narrative of power dynamics and influencing the course of political events. By understanding the sources and expressions of power, campaign managers can create messages that resonate with voters and shape political perceptions.

Chapter 7

Case Study

BOTH ROOSEVELT AND THATCHER, despite their differing political ideologies and historical contexts, exemplified how a deep understanding of governance and strategic action can be used to influence their political destiny and achieve legitimacy and authority in their respective eras.

Franklin D. Roosevelt (FDR): FDR demonstrated an exceptional understanding of governance. He utilized the executive powers of the presidency to an unprecedented extent, initiating the New Deal, a series of programs, public work projects, financial reforms, and regulations.

Margaret Thatcher: Thatcher had a deep understanding of the institutional mechanisms of the British government. She used this knowledge to implement widespread reforms.

Part Two

The Critical Decision

To Run or Not to Run?

Deciding whether to run for political office is a complex and deeply personal decision that involves weighing numerous self-assessment factors.

Chapter 8

Introspective Self-Assessment

Are You Ready?

EVALUATE YOURSELF: This introspection is crucial for understanding your readiness and capability to serve effectively. Consider if your experiences and skills align with the responsibilities of the position. Identify areas where you need improvement or support, reflect on your strengths, weaknesses, and qualifications for the office you're considering.

• **Clarify Your Goals**: Your goals should reflect a commitment to public service and community betterment. Clearly define your motivations and the specific impact you aim to achieve. Outline the changes or improvements you wish to enact, ensuring they resonate with the community's needs and priorities.

• **Family Support**: Their support is a crucial pillar of strength throughout your political endeavor because campaigning and serving in office demands significant time and energy, which can strain personal relationships. That's why having open and candid conversations with your family about the sacrifices and challenges ahead are vitally important.

Chapter 9

The Smell Test
Evaluating Candidacy Viability

THIS TEST ISN'T A WRITTEN or verbal exam it's about embodying values and ethical principles that resonate deeply with the public and the demands of the office. This journey requires unwavering commitment to integrity, transparency, and accountability.

• **Triumph over Adversity**: As you navigate the political arena, remember that the media's tales of scandal are tests of your character. Face these tests with the courage, conviction and truth. Uphold your values, remain transparent, and be accountable for in all of your actions. In doing so, you will not only pass the smell test but also emerge as a beacon of hope and integrity in the tumultuous world of politics.

• **Effective Leadership:** Political incumbents and challengers alike guide their constituents toward shared goals with vision, courage, and integrity. Their leadership qualities should be second to none embodying the type of personal qualities that captivates and empowers all whom they lead.

• **Embrace Potential**: For political incumbents and challengers, the path to leadership is a call to action, a challenge to transcend the ordinary and achieve the extraordinary. By leading - by example - inspiring and motivating others, your journey has the power to reshape the future, ignite the hearts of your constituents, and forge a path to a brighter more prosperous tomorrow.

Chapter 10

Understanding the Political Landscape

ANALYZE THE ENVIRONMENT: Whether incumbent or challenger, dive deep into the current political climate of your community or district. A comprehensive understanding of the political landscape will strengthen your campaigns strategy and help you connect with voters on key issues.

• **Resources and Finances**: Financial stability and robust support networks are essential for sustaining your campaign from start to finish. Assess whether you have access to these resources independently or can garner external support. This includes considering your fundraising abilities, campaign infrastructure, and the significant commitment time needed.

• **Risk Assessment**: A proactive approach to risk management will fortify your resolve and readiness to overcome adversities. Conduct a thorough evaluation of the risks involved in pursuing political office. Understand that challenges, including electoral defeat or public scrutiny, are part and parcel of any political journey. You must be prepared to face setbacks and obstacles with relentless determination.

• **Long-Term Vision**: A forward-thinking vision will guide your policies and initiatives, ensuring you have a lasting positive impact. Consider the legacy you aspire to leave and how your decisions and actions will shape your community and the broader political landscape. Think beyond the immediate election and envision the long-term implications of holding public office.

• **Triumph over Adversity**: As you navigate the political arena, remember that the media's tales of scandal are tests of your character. Face these tests with the courage and conviction and truth, uphold your values, remain transparent, and be accountable for all of your actions. In doing so, you will not only pass the smell test but also emerge as a beacon of hope and integrity in the tumultuous world of politics.

Chapter 11

Case Study

Both Joe Biden and Hillary Clinton's decisions to run for president illustrate the multifaceted nature of such a decision, involving personal, familial, health, and political considerations.

Joe Biden:

Joe Biden's decision to run for the presidency in the 2020 election was marked by significant personal and professional considerations.

• Self-assessment Factors: Family Considerations: Biden's family played a crucial role in his decision-making. His son Beau's death in 2015 profoundly affected him, and his family's support was pivotal in his decision to run.

• Political Climate: The political environment and the perceived threat to democratic norms under the Trump administration motivated Biden. He believed he could unite the country and restore dignity to the presidency.

• Health and Age: At 77, Biden had to consider his age and health, evaluating whether he had the physical and mental stamina for the rigorous demands of a presidential campaign and potentially serving as president.

Hillary Clinton:

Hillary Clinton's decision to run for president in the 2016 election involved intricate deliberations influenced by her extensive political career and personal history.

• Self-assessment Factors: Legacy and Experience: Clinton assessed her extensive experience in public service, including her roles as First Lady, U.S. Senator, and Secretary of State, and how these roles prepared her for the presidency.

• Public Perception: She had to weigh her controversial public image and the intense scrutiny she faced from both supporters and detractors.

• Personal Ambition vs. Public Service: Clinton balanced her personal ambition and long-held aspiration to become the first female president against the potential impact on her family, particularly the media attention on her daughter Chelsea and husband Bill Clinton.

Political Landscape: The political landscape, including the potential competitors and the issues facing the country, played a crucial role in her decision. She believed her vision and policies were essential for the progress of the nation.

Part Three

Crafting Resonant Campaign Messages

In politics, one message does not fit all. You must craft several effective, common-senses, emotionally appealing messages that resonate with voters and inspires them to take action.

Chapter 12

Building Message Structure

Frameworks for Success

Use an inspiring tone and motivational content to energize your supporters and boost their enthusiasm for your candidacy. Your message should have a sharp focus, if the goal is to rally support for your campaign, emphasize community values and the positive impact your policies will have on all residents.

• **Audience Understanding**: Tailor your message to address your audience specific concerns and priorities. For example, if you're addressing a community worried about environmental issues, highlight your commitment to sustainability and protecting local ecosystems. Knowing your audience is crucial.

• **Simple and Memorable Slogan**: A concise, easy-to-remember slogan effectively communicates your key points to voters. A powerful slogan like "the right to live free from violence and discrimination" summarize your commitment to both non-violence and women's rights.

• **Emotional Appeal**: Depending upon your main objective use emotion to paint a clear verbal picture. Share personal stories to highlight the impact of your policies and how by adopting them a brighter tomorrow is just a vote away.

• **Common Sense Logic**: Speak plainly and avoid jargon to ensure your message is accessible and persuasive to all voters. Support your platform message with evidence-based arguments, such as performance statistics.

• **Solution-Oriented**: Present concrete proposals for sustainable practices to improve current circumstances. By offering actionable solutions, you show your commitment to addressing challenges rather than just highlighting problems.

• **Authenticity and Trustworthiness**: Be genuine in your communication. Avoid overstating or making false promises. Transparency builds trust with voters, so be honest about the limitations of your policies while emphasizing your dedication to their interests.

• **Call to Action**: Encourage voters to support your campaign through volunteering, donating, or spreading the word. Clearly outline how they can get involved and make a difference in the community.

• **Repetition and Consistency**: Reinforce your message across various platforms, social media, campaign events, and literature. Consistent repetition solidifies your brand identity and ensures your key points are effectively communicated to voters.

• **Adaptability**: Stay flexible and responsive to feedback and changing circumstances. Be prepared to adjust your messaging to address new issues as they arise, maintaining relevance with your audience.

Chapter 13

Defining Platform Core Elements
Anchoring Your Campaign

WHETHER YOU ARE AN INCUMBENT, a challenger, or a campaign manager, the narrative you craft can be the decisive factor in winning or losing an election.

• **Policy Positions**: These should be meticulously defined, practical, and firmly rooted in your core values. They are the cornerstone of your campaign, laying out specific proposals and plans to address the most pressing issues in your community / region.

• **Economic Prosperity for All**: Propose initiatives that stimulate job creation, support small businesses, and ensure fair wages. Articulate a vision of an economy that works for everyone, not just the privileged few. Highlight how these policies will improve the everyday lives of your constituents, from lower taxes to enhanced social programs.

• **Healthcare for a Healthier Nation**: Whether it's expanding Medicaid, introducing public options, or controlling prescription drug prices, demonstrate your commitment to keeping families healthy and secure. Present a comprehensive plan to ensure affordable and accessible healthcare for all.

• **Education that Empowers**: Emphasize policies that support public schools, reduce student debt, and promote life-long learning opportunities. Advocate for an education system that equips students with the skills needed for now and the future.

• **A Sustainable Environment**: This could include investing in renewable energy, reducing carbon emissions, and preserving natural resources for future generations. Showcase your commitment to protecting the planet with actionable steps towards sustainability.

• **Foreign Policy that Promotes Peace and Security**: Stress the importance of alliances, international cooperation, and a commitment to human rights. Outline a strategy for engaging with the world that balances national security with diplomatic efforts

• **Social Justice and Equality**: Whether its civil rights, criminal justice reform, affordable housing, or LGBTQ+ rights, show that you stand for justice and equality for all. Address social issues head-on by proposing measures that tackle systemic inequality and promote fairness.

• **Simple and Memorable Slogan**: A concise, easy-to-remember slogan effectively communicates your key points to voters. A powerful slogan like "the right to live free from violence and discrimination" summarizes your commitment to both non-violence and women's rights.

Chapter 14

Setting Message Priorities

What Matters Most

YOUR PRIORITIES REFLECT the most urgent and significant issues your campaign aims to tackle upon assuming office. Identifying and communicating these priorities effectively can demonstrate your leadership and resolve.

• **Immediate Crisis Management**: Show voters that you are prepared to lead through crises with competence and care. Whether it's a public health crisis, economic downturn, or environmental disaster, prioritize immediate action plans to manage and mitigate the impact.

• **Neglected Issues That Need Attention**: This could be anything from infrastructure improvements to veterans' services. Shine a light on issues that have been overlooked or neglected by current leadership. By addressing these, you prove that you are in tune with the needs of the community.

Innovative Solutions for Long-Standing Problems: Shows that you are a proactive and visionary person. Bring forward fresh, innovative solutions to age-old problems. For instance, introduce groundbreaking policies on renewable energy, digital transformation in public services, or new educational methodologies.

Chapter 15

Weaving a Compelling Narrative
Engaging Hearts and Minds

To MAKE issues and concerns truly compelling, weave them into a narrative that are personal, relatable, and forward-looking.

- **Personal Stories**: Share stories of individuals who have been affected by the issues you aim to address, making your platform more relatable and impactful. Use anecdotes and personal stories to humanize your policy positions.

- **Inspiring Vision**: Use vivid, positive imagery to help voters imagine the better world your policies will create. Paint a picture of the future you envision

Chapter 16

Case Study

BARACK OBAMA and Narendra Modi demonstrated that effective political messaging involves crafting narratives that resonate emotionally and address the specific needs and aspirations of diverse voter groups. Their ability to inspire action through tailored, emotionally appealing messages underscores the importance of nuanced communication in political campaigns.

Barack Obama Campaigns: 2008 and 2012 U.S. Presidential Elections

Obama's message inspired record voter turnout, particularly among young people and minority groups, and his ability to connect emotionally with diverse audiences was a key factor in his electoral success.

Narendra Modi Campaigns: 2014 and 2019 Indian General Elections

Modi's ability to craft a message that appealed to both the aspirational middle class and the traditional rural voters played a significant role in his overwhelming electoral victories. His campaigns effectively mobilized a wide base of support, translating into significant political success.

50

Part Four

Building a Formidable Campaign Team

Creating an unbeatable political campaign team requires a meticulous blend of essential elements that forge a strong, cohesive, and effective unit. Build a powerhouse team ready to navigate the complex political landscape and achieve victory.

Chapter 17

Key Components for Success
Essential Roles and Responsibilities

• **SHARED VISION AND VALUES:** Unity in vision stimulates coherence and a sense of belonging, making the team stronger and more focused. This common purpose bolsters team spirit and ensures a consistent, compelling message is delivered to supporters and voters.

• **Diverse Skill Sets:** Each member's unique perspective and strength contributes to a holistic approach to campaign operations. By incorporating talents from various fields (campaign strategy, communications, fundraising, data analysis, grassroots organizing, and digital media) the team gains a comprehensive edge, enhancing its ability to address every facet of the campaign.

• **Strong Leadership:** Setting the tone, provides clear direction, and empowers team members to perform at their best in the face of challenges, resilient leadership keeps the team focused and motivate. To make a long story short, strong leaders inspire, communicate effectively, make strategic decisions, and manage resources.

• **Clear Roles and Responsibilities**: Each team

member must understand their specific duties to prevent duplication of efforts and ensure timely completion of tasks. Clear delineation of roles encourages a culture of ownership, minimizes confusion, and streamlines workflow, inevitably driving the team towards its objectives with precision.

• **Effective Communication:** Establishing clear channels for regular updates, meetings, and feedback ensures that the team stays informed and aligned with the campaign's goals. It promotes collaboration, resolves conflicts, and strengthens relationships, enhancing overall cohesion and productivity.

• **Strategic Planning and Execution:** Strategic planning and precise execution keep the campaign on track and responsive to evolving circumstances. Breaking down the strategy into actionable tasks and projects ensures systematic execution. By setting clear goals, timelines, and milestones, the team can maintain focus and adapt to changes with agility and purpose.

• **Adaptability and Flexibility**: In the ever-changing world of politics, adaptability is crucial. A team that can pivot quickly in response to new challenges and opportunities maintains a competitive edge. Embracing flexibility and innovation allows the team to adjust tactics and strategies, ensuring it can navigate the dynamic political landscape effectively.

• **Resource Mobilization**: Effective fundraising and resource management provide the means to reach and engage voters. Mobilizing resources such as funding, volunteers, endorsements, and media support is vital for sustaining a competitive campaign. To that end, building strong networks within the community and beyond enhances resource mobilization efforts, ensuring the campaign's strength and reach

• **Data-Driven Decision Making:** Leveraging data and analytics is essential for informed decision-making. Data-driven approaches allow the campaign to measure progress, identify improvement areas, and adjust strategies for maximum effectiveness. By analyzing demographics, optimizing messaging, and efficiently allocating resources, the team enhances its competitiveness and impact.

• **Empathy and Relatability**: Genuine empathy promotes nurtures bonds between the campaign and its supporters, increasing engagement and loyalty. Cultivating empathy and relatability with voters builds trust and connection. Understanding voters' concerns and aspirations allows the team to craft messages that resonate personally, forging a deeper connection with the electorate.

• **Commitment to Ethical Conduct:** Maintaining high ethical standards is fundamental to building trust and credibility. Transparency, honesty, and accountability in all campaign aspects strengthen confidence in its leadership and mission. A commitment to ethical conduct earns respect and support, enhancing the campaign's reputation and chances of success.

Chapter 18

Optimal Team Structure

Organizing for Efficiency

THE POWER of ideas and the art of storytelling are paramount in capturing the hearts and minds of voters.

The Candidate

At the heart of every campaign is the candidate – the individual whose vision, values, and leadership qualities seek to inspire and win the trust of voters. The candidate's charisma, relatability, and ability to connect with constituents are fundamental to driving the campaign's message forward.

The Campaign Manager

The campaign manager's leadership and organizational skills are vital in keeping the campaign on track. This role involves coordinating the efforts of the entire team, managing day-to-day operations, and ensuring that every aspect of the campaign is aligned with the overarching goals. This person is the mastermind behind the campaign's strategy and execution.

The Communications Director

The communications director ensures that the candidate's voice is consistent, compelling, and reaches the intended audience effectively. This role encompasses managing all communication channels, including media relations, social media, and advertising. Crafting compelling campaign messages is the responsibility of the communications director.

The Field Organizer / Director

The field director / organizer is the engine behind voter outreach efforts. From organizing door-to-door canvassing, phone banking to recruiting and mobilizing volunteers; this person's role is to build a robust ground game creating a personal connection with district residents.

The Finance Director

Fundraising is the lifeblood of any campaign, and the finance director is at the helm of these efforts. This role involves managing donor relations, planning fundraising events, and overseeing the campaign's budget. The finance director's ability to secure financial resources ensures the campaign has the necessary funds to operate effectively throughout the campaign process.

The Policy Advisor

This role involves researching and providing insights on various policy issues, helping the candidate formulate positions that resonate with voters. The policy advisor's work is crucial in establishing the candidate as knowledgeable and credible on key issues.

The Digital Director

The digital director oversees the campaign's website, email marketing, and social media strategy. A strong online presence is indispensable and by leveraging digital tools, this role amplifies the campaign's message, engages with a broader audience, and mobilizes online supporters.

The Pollster/Strategist

This role ensures the campaign remains responsive to voter sentiments and can adapt to changing dynamics.

The Volunteer Coordinator

A well-organized volunteer force can significantly amplify the campaign's reach and impact. The volunteer coordinator works with the campaign field director to recruit, train, and manage volunteers, ensuring they are motivated and equipped to support the campaign's activities.

The Legal Advisor

This role provides crucial guidance on legal matters, ensuring that the campaign operates within the bounds of the law and avoids potential pitfalls. Navigating complex campaign finance laws and compliance issues is the domain of the legal advisor.

Chapter 19

Compensation Strategies
Motivating Your Team

FROM ALLOCATING resources to attracting top talent, the way you manage your campaign team's pay can significantly influence your success. In the high-stakes world of political campaigns, every decision matters.

• **Resource Allocation**: Balancing Budgets for Maximum Impact

Campaigns often operate under tight budget constraints, making it essential to allocate resources wisely. Each dollar spent on salaries is one less dollar for advertising, outreach, or voter engagement. Striking a balance ensures all facets of the campaign are supported, maintaining a cohesive and effective strategy.

• **Cost Efficiency:** efficient use of funds starts with identifying which roles are crucial to your campaign's success. For high-stakes races, investing in a seasoned campaign manager, even at a higher salary, can be pivotal. Their strategic insight and experience can drive the campaign's overall coherence and execution, ultimately saving money by enhancing efficiency.

- **Skill Assessment**: not all campaign roles are created equal. High-level positions like campaign manager or communications director require significant experience and strategic acumen, justifying higher salaries. Properly assessing the skills needed for each role ensures that your team is well-equipped to handle the campaign's demands.

- **Impact Evaluation:** Evaluate the impact of each role on the campaign's success. Positions that directly influence voter outreach, fundraising, and media strategy are critical and may warrant higher compensation. By focusing resources on these high-impact areas, you can drive greater overall success.

- **Staying Competitive**: To attract and retain top talent, competitive pay is essential. Analyzing market rates for similar positions in other campaigns or industries provides benchmarks for setting salaries. This ensures you're offering attractive packages that draw skilled professionals to your team.

- **Value Recognition**: Fair compensation is more than just competitive rates; it's about recognizing the value each team member brings. Ensuring fair pay promotes loyalty, motivation, and a sense of equity, which translates into a more dedicated and effective team.

- **Ethical Considerations**: Ethical considerations are vital in compensation decisions. Paying fair wages aligns with your campaign's values and promotes a positive organizational culture. This ethical approach not only boosts team morale but also enhances your campaign's public image.

Chapter 20

The Perfect Recruitment Questionnaire

Finding the Right Fit

THIS RECRUITMENT QUESTIONNAIRE is a gateway to a campaign fueled by passion, innovation, and unwavering commitment to change. All members of the core team should answer the following questions;

• **What Motivates You?** As it relates to politics -what deep-rooted yearning for tangible, impactful change are you seeking?

• **A Moment of Political Impact:** Reflect on a pivotal instant where politics ceased to be a distant concept and became something you needed to make sure your voice was heard?

• **Envisioning Tomorrow**: In words paint a vivid picture of the future that reflects how the community has improved because of your involvement with this campaign.

• **Embracing the Unexpected:** Address how you confront unforeseen challenges and obstacles and proceed ahead, undeterred.

• **Unleashing Your Talents**: Identify the unique gifts

you bring to the table and how they align with our campaign's objectives.

• **Cost Efficiency:** Efficient use of funds starts with identifying which roles are crucial to your campaign's success. For high-stakes races, investing in a seasoned campaign manager, even at a higher salary, can be pivotal. Their strategic insight and experience can drive the campaign's overall coherence and execution, ultimately saving money by enhancing efficiency.

• **Skill Assessment**: Not all campaign roles are created equal. High-level positions like campaign manager or communications director require significant experience and strategic acumen, justifying higher salaries. Properly assessing the skills needed for each role ensures that your team is well-equipped to handle the campaign's demands.

• **Impact Evaluation:** Evaluate the impact of each role on the campaign's success.

Positions that directly influence voter outreach, fundraising, and media strategy are

critical and may warrant higher compensation. By focusing resources on these

high-impact areas can drive greater overall success.

Chapter 21

Case Study

BOTH BARACK OBAMA and Bill Clinton built campaign teams that were not only effective but also innovative, setting new standards in political campaigning through their strategic, data-driven, and cohesive approaches.

Barack Obama: Campaign Team:

• David Plouffe (Campaign Manager): Plouffe was known for his strategic acumen and played a pivotal role in orchestrating the overall campaign strategy.

• David Axelrod (Chief Strategist): Axelrod's deep understanding of political messaging and communication helped shape Obama's public image and policy messages.

• Robert Gibbs (Communications Director): Gibbs managed the campaign's communication strategy, ensuring consistent and clear messaging.

• Jim Messina (Chief of Staff): Messina coordinated the campaign's various operations, ensuring that all parts of the team worked together seamlessly.

• Stephanie Cutter (Deputy Campaign Manager): Cutter

focused on rapid response and strategic communication, effectively countering opponent attacks.

Bill Clinton: Campaign Team:

• James Carville (Lead Strategist): Carville's sharp political instincts and ability to distill complex issues into simple, compelling messages were crucial.

• Paul Begala (Advisor): Begala worked closely with Carville to craft and implement the campaign's strategy.

• George Stephanopoulos (Communications Director): Stephanopoulos handled the campaign's media relations and communication strategies.

• Dee Dee Myers (Press Secretary): Myers managed press relations, ensuring that the campaign's narrative was effectively communicated to the public.

• Mickey Kantor (Campaign Chairman): Kantor oversaw the overall campaign operations, ensuring coordination and effectiveness.

Part Five

Innovative Fundraising Tactics

In the fast-paced world of politics, securing a steady stream of funds is the lifeline that sustains any campaign. Traditional tactics alone won't suffice in an evolving landscape. It's time to unearth innovative strategies that captivate donors and fuel the momentum needed to clinch victory.

Chapter 22

Strategic Fundraising Elements

Planning for Success

STRATEGIC ELEMENTS:

Donor-Centricity: This approach cultivates connections that transcend mere transactions, creating bonds grounded in shared values and mutual respect. By understanding donors' motivations and aspirations, you can tailor appeals that resonate deeply.

• **Transparency:** Donors seek assurance that their contributions will lead to meaningful change. Clarity is paramount. By being open about your goals and aspirations, you build credibility and trust.

• **Nurturing Relationships**: Through genuine expressions of gratitude and personalized interactions, you cultivate a community united by a common purpose.

• **Relevance**: This sparks a groundswell of support that cannot be ignored. Aligning your campaign cause with current public sentiment ensures your message resonates widely.

• **Impact**: Demonstrating the tangible difference every dollar makes through compelling storytelling and real-world examples breathes life into your campaign cause.

• **Diversification:** Casting wide nets safeguards against uncertainty. By tapping into a rich tapestry of supporters and resources, you sustain your campaign efforts through every twist and turn.

• **Stewardship**: Honoring the trust bestowed upon us through unwavering transparency and open communication ensures every donor feels valued.

• **Persistence**: Your campaign's strength lies in your unwavering resolve to press on, undeterred by challenges.

• **Flexibility**: Embracing adaptability allows you to evolve in the face of change, ensuring your campaign remains innovative and forward-thinking.

Chapter 23

Proven Fundraising Methods

Techniques that Work

Crowdfunding Platforms: Platforms like *ActBlue*, *WinRed*, and *GoFundMe* democratize support, tapping into the collective strength of everyday individuals.

- **Individual Donations**: Building a robust grassroots base through heartfelt direct mail campaigns, personal phone calls, and face-to-face interactions forges meaningful connections.

- **Online Fundraising**: Leveraging social media, email newsletters, and dedicated fundraising websites extend reach and simplify the donation process.

- **Fundraising Events**: Events like galas or intimate dinners provide platforms to showcase the candidate's vision and express gratitude.

- **Phone-a-Thons**: Personal calls offer a unique opportunity to connect directly with potential donors, forging genuine connections.

- **Peer-to-Peer Fundraising**: Empowering supporters to become champions for the cause taps into vast networks of potential donors.

- **Major Donor Cultivation**: Cultivating relationships with major donors requires personalized outreach and genuine stewardship for long-term impact.
- **Direct Mail Campaigns**: Well-crafted mailers offer tangible touchpoints, connecting with older demographics and niche donor segments.
- **Grassroots Fundraising Drives**: Local engagement through door-to-door canvassing and neighborhood meet-and-greets mobilizes volunteers to advocate for change.
- **Corporate Donations**: Ensuring alignment with corporate donors' values and maintaining ethical standards is crucial for forging beneficial partnerships.
- **Transparency**: Donors seek assurance that their contributions will lead to meaningful change. Clarity is paramount, being open about your goals and aspirations build trust and credibility.
- **Stewardship:** Honoring the trust bestowed upon you through unwavering transparency and open communication ensures every donor feels valued.

Chapter 24

Compliance and Record Keeping
Staying Legal and Organized

UNDERSTANDING CAMPAIGN FINANCE LAWS: Regular review of federal, state, and local regulations is essential for compliance.

• **Transparency and Accountability**: Proper record-keeping ensures all financial transactions are documented accurately, maintaining trust with donors and the public.

• **Building Trust**: Demonstrating a commitment to compliance and ethical conduct builds trust with stakeholders.

• **Risk Mitigation**: Proactive compliance and robust record-keeping practices mitigate risks and protect the campaign's reputation.

Chapter 25

Follow-Up and Acknowledgment
Building Donor Relationships

GRATITUDE AND APPRECIATION: Expressing genuine gratitude recognizes the significance of every contribution, fostering a deeper connection with supporters.

• **Personalization**: Personalized thank-you notes, emails, or phone calls transform transactions into meaningful relationships, making each donor feel valued.

• **Nurturing Relationships**: Keeping donors informed about the impact of their contributions nurtures long-term connections built on trust and transparency.

• **Encouraging Future Support**: Highlighting upcoming opportunities for involvement and reinforcing the value of past contributions encourages ongoing support.

Chapter 26

Case Study

Bernie Sanders' and Barack Obama both illustrated how innovative fundraising strategies can secure a steady stream of funds in the fast-paced world of politics, ensuring their campaigns remained financially viable and competitive.

Bernie Sanders' presidential campaigns in 2016 and 2020 showcased the power of crowdsourced funding, relying heavily on small-dollar donations and a fervent base of supporters. Sanders' reliance on small-dollar donations proved highly effective, allowing him to remain competitive despite not having the backing of large donors or super PACs. In 2016, Sanders raised over \$230 million, with an average donation of \$27. In 2020, he continued to draw substantial funds from a wide base of small donors, maintaining financial viability throughout the primary season.

Barack Obama's 2008 presidential campaign is a landmark example of successful political fundraising, particularly through the use of online platforms and social media. The campaign leveraged the power of the internet to reach a vast number of small donors, transforming the traditional fundraising model. Obama's innovative use of technology and grassroots fundraising enabled his campaign to raise over $750 million, a record-breaking amount at the time. This financial strength allowed the campaign to invest heavily in advertising, field operations, and voter outreach, ultimately contributing to his victory.

Part Six

Mobilizing a Groundswell of Supporters

Mobilizing people requires a cause your campaign platform and you – the candidate – must envision and present an effective cause.

Chapter 27

Defining the Cause
Rallying Behind a Vision

At the heart of every mobilization effort lays a crystal-clear purpose. Define your purpose with unwavering clarity—let it be the beacon that shows supporters not just what you stand for, but why their involvement is indispensable.

- **Inclusivity**: In the unity of our differences lies the strength to overcome any challenge and build a movement reflecting humanity's richness. Embracing diversity is your greatest asset, creating a space where every voice is heard and valued.

- **Engagement**: Start a discussion that invites them to become co-creators of the narrative, sowing the seeds of community and collective action. Engage with your audience on every front, from bustling streets to the digital realm.

- **Empowerment:** Delegate and nurture leadership at every level of your movement, equipping your supporters with the tools and support they need to become agents of transformation. Empower individuals to become architects of change.

Inspiration: Weave tales of triumph and resilience that

resonate deeply, kindling the flame of inspiration and lighting the path toward a brighter future. Paint a vision of tomorrow that ignites the imagination.

Chapter 28

Effective Organizational Structure

ADAPTATION: Flexibility and agility are essential for maintaining momentum and relevance. Be adaptable and responsive to changing circumstances, opportunities, and challenges.

ENGAGEMENT: Engage with your audience on every front, from bustling streets to the digital realm. Start a discussion that invites voters to become co-creators of the narrative, sowing the seeds of community and collective action.

• **Strategic Alliances**: Collaborative efforts can amplify impact, broaden reach, and leverage resources effectively. Forge strategic alliances and partnerships with like-minded organizations, groups, and individuals.

• **Sustained Action**: Nurture relationships, encourage a sense of community, and celebrate milestones and achievements. Maintain enthusiasm and commitment among supporters through regular communication, ongoing activities, and recognition of contributions

Chapter 29

Mobilization Tools

Equipping Your Advocates

LEVERAGE TECHNOLOGY TO mobilize people efficiently, expand outreach, and facilitate communication and coordination. Utilize tools such as social media, online forums, and mobile apps to streamline organizing efforts and reach a broader audience.

- **Voter Contact Management Software:** Use platforms like NGP VAN or Nation Builder to track engagement with voters, volunteers, and donors. These tools help campaigns manage voter data and interactions, allowing for strategic outreach based on real-time data.

- **Mobile Canvassing Apps**: Apps like Minivan or Canvasser empower volunteers with digital tools to streamline canvassing, record voter responses, and input feedback in real-time, enhancing data accuracy and immediacy.

- **Walk Lists and Scripts**: Standardize canvassing efforts to ensure consistency in message delivery and data collection. Provide volunteers with these resources to maintain coherence in outreach strategies and assess performance.

- **Digital Dashboards**: Offer campaign manager's real-

85

time insights into canvassing activities, enabling informed decision-making. Customize dashboards to track key performance indicators (KPIs) and identify areas for improvement.

• **Performance Metrics and Analytics**: Define performance metrics to assess the effectiveness of canvassing activities. Analyse data from voter interactions to identify trends, evaluate performance, and continually optimize outreach strategies.

• **Sustained Action**: Nurture relationships, encourage a sense of community, celebrate milestones and achievements. Maintain enthusiasm and commitment among supporters through regular communication, ongoing activities, and recognition of contributions.

Chapter 30

Quality Assurance
Maintaining Standards

PROVIDE volunteers with training and feedback mechanisms to foster continuous improvement in canvassing skills and performance. Conduct debriefing sessions and share best practices.

• **Performance Incentives and Recognition**: Motivate volunteers through performance incentives and recognition. Acknowledge top performers and offer rewards for achieving specific goals to inspire continued dedication.

• **Continuous Improvement Processes**: Regularly evaluate and refine canvassing strategies based on feedback, performance data, and outcomes. Assess the effectiveness of tools and processes, and replicate successful approaches to elevate campaign performance.

• **Leverage technology**: To mobilize people efficiently, expand community outreach connections by utilizing mobile apps to streamline organizing efforts thereby reaching a broader audience quick, faster and effetely.

Chapter 31

Igniting Voter Engagement
Turning Interest into Action

PROVIDE a direct conduit for candidates to engage with the electorate. These gatherings cultivate transparency and accessibility, allowing candidates to listen to the community's concerns and aspirations.

• **Targeted Advertising**: Use precision to craft messages that resonate deeply within specific demographics and geographic enclaves. Speak directly to the hearts and minds of those who matter most.

• **Community Outreach Events**: Participate in parades, festivals, and local fairs to connect with voters on a personal level. These events help earn trust through genuine interactions.

• **Volunteer Mobilization**: Leverage the efforts of volunteers to extend the reach of campaigns. From voter registration drives to door-to-door canvassing, volunteers transform apathy into action.

• **Interactive Campaign Tools**: Use quizzes, surveys, and interactive maps to engage voters. These tools offer avenues for expression and empowerment, allowing voters to shape the discourse in real-time.

90

Chapter 32

Building Meaningful Relationships

Sustaining Support

REVEAL your genuine core beneath political rhetoric. Authenticity builds trust and credibility, rallying supporters behind your cause.

- **Respect:** Treat others with dignity and grace. Respectful communication leads to understanding and collaboration across diverse demographics.

- **Empathy**: Step into voters' shoes to understand their concerns. Empathy breeds trust and engagement.

- **Communication:** Be transparent, honest, and clear in your communication. Trust flourishes in an open environment, enabling conflicts to be resolved gracefully.

- **Listening**: Practice active listening. Give undivided attention and validate concerns to build strong relationships.

- **Boundaries:** Respect personal and professional boundaries. Honoring boundaries minimizes misunderstandings and conflicts.

- **Reciprocity**: Give as much as you receive. Acts of kindness and support strengthen bonds.

- **Reliability**: Follow through on commitments. Reliability breeds confidence and ensures continued support.
- **Networking**: Cultivate a diverse network of connections. Networking opens doors to new opportunities and alliances.
- **Gratitude**: Express appreciation for contributions and support. Gratitude fosters camaraderie among allies.
- **Integrity**: Uphold honesty, ethics, and moral principles. Integrity is the foundation of lasting relationships.
- **Professionalism**: Maintain professionalism in all interactions. Respect, integrity, and credibility solidify your image as a trustworthy leader.

Chapter 33

Embracing Community Wisdom
Listening and Learning

INCUMBENTS: Move from complacency to renewal. Engage with the community actively to bridge gaps and unlock untapped potential. Embrace diverse perspectives to enrich governance.

Challengers: Ignite a collective spark for change. Draw strength from the community's collective intelligence and transform aspirations into tangible progress through dialogue, coalition-building, and empowerment.

Authenticity: Build trust and credibility by rallying supporters behind your cause.

Chapter 34

Case Study

Barack Obama and Brexit Campaign both campaigns demonstrate how a clear, compelling cause—whether it is hope and change or national sovereignty—can effectively mobilize people when paired with a strategic and inclusive approach.

Barack Obama's 2008 Presidential Campaign - Cause: "Hope and Change"

Campaign Platform and Candidate: Barack Obama ran on a platform promising hope and change, which resonated deeply with a wide range of voters, particularly young people, minorities, and disillusioned voters who were tired of the status quo. His campaign emphasized themes of unity, progress, and the need for a new direction in American politics after years of war and economic instability.

Brexit Campaign (Vote Leave) in the 2016 United Kingdom EU Referendum - Cause: "Take Back Control"

Campaign Platform and Candidate: The Vote Leave campaign advocated for the United Kingdom to leave the European Union. The platform focused on regaining sovereignty, controlling immigration, and redirecting funds from the EU to domestic priorities like the National Health Service (NHS). Key figures in the campaign included politicians like Boris Johnson and Michael Gove, who argued that Brexit would restore the UK's independence and democracy.

Part Seven

Harnessing the Power of Social Media

To effectively utilize social media for strategic advantage requires wisdom and foresight to navigate the digital landscape.

Chapter 35

Key Strategies

Maximizing Online Presence

• **KNOW YOUR AUDIENCE**: Dive deep into the psyche of your target demographic. Understand their digital footprint, preferences, and passions. Craft content that speaks directly to their hearts, elevating a profound connection that transcends the digital divide.

• **Engage with Compelling Content**: Captivate your audience with a rich tapestry of multimedia content. From captivating images to interactive polls, each piece should be a masterpiece. Whether informative, entertaining, or emotionally stirring, let your content captivate and resonate.

• **Visual Allure**: Paint a vivid picture with high-quality images and videos. Let your visuals speak volumes, drawing in viewers and compelling them to share your message across social platforms.

• **Master the Art of Storytelling**: Humanize your brand with personal anecdotes, user-generated content and heartfelt testimonials. Weave narratives that tug at the heartstrings, forging an emotional bond that transcends mere pixels on a screen.

- **Consistency is Key**: Maintain a steady drumbeat of content. Utilize scheduling tools to ensure a consistent flow, keeping your audience engaged and eager for more.
- **Engaging Dialogue:** Cultivate a vibrant community by engaging in two-way communication. Listen to your audience, respond promptly, and nurture a sense of belonging. Let your followers know they're valued participants in a larger conversation.
- **Strategic Hashtag Deployment**: Harness the power of hashtags to amplify your message. Choose wisely, incorporating relevant tags that boost discoverability and extend your reach within the vast digital ecosystem.
- **Monitor and Adapt**: Stay ahead of the curve by monitoring analytics and adapting to evolving trends. Experiment with new features, analyze performance metrics, and refine your strategy to stay ahead of the curve.
- **Build a Thriving Community**: Advance a sense of solidarity among your followers. Encourage user-generated content, host interactive sessions, and promote a culture of collaboration and inclusion.
- **Collaborate for Impact**: Join forces with like-minded influencers, brands, and organizations. Collaborative efforts amplify your message, broaden your reach, and solidify your influence in the digital arena.

Chapter 36

Building Brand Awareness
Making Your Mark

WHETHER YOU'RE an incumbent defending your seat or a challenger aiming to disrupt the status quo, the principles of brand awareness are your secret weapon. With the right strategy, you can transform your political persona into a compelling narrative that resonates with voters.

- **Share Your Background and Personal** Journey: People connect with stories, not just statistics. Whether it's overcoming adversity or a lifelong commitment to public service, your story should inspire and resonate on a human level.

- **Identify Your Villains and Allies:** Villains: Identify the issues and challenges facing your community. These are the enemies in your narrative. Allies: Showcase endorsements and partnerships. Highlight community leaders, organizations, and influential figures that support your vision.

- **Visual Storytelling**: Utilize videos and images to tell your story. Behind-the-scenes glimpses, campaign trail highlights, and personal anecdotes humanize your campaign.

Chapter 37

Case Study

Barack Obama and Donald Trump campaigns illustrate the power of social media in modern political strategy, highlighting different approaches and their respective impacts on electoral success.

Barack Obama's 2008 Presidential Campaign: The use of social media helped Obama build a broad and energized supporter base, particularly among younger voters. The campaign's innovative digital strategy is credited with helping secure his victory in the 2008 election.

Donald Trump's 2016 Presidential Campaign: Trump's adept use of social media allowed him to build a passionate and engaged base of supporters, maintain constant media coverage, and effectively counter negative news stories. His direct and unfiltered communication style resonated with many voters, contributing significantly to his electoral victory in 2016.

Part Eight

The Enduring Value of Traditional Media

While digital platforms undoubtedly play a pivotal role in campaigning, overlooking the influence of newspapers, radio, and television would be a grave mistake. These time-honored channels possess a unique ability to reach demographics that may not be active online, broadening a candidate's exposure and solidifying their presence in the public consciousness.

Chapter 38

Timeless Tools for Communication

Leveraging Established Channels

ADHERENCE to traditional media deadlines is paramount. Seasoned incumbents and bold challengers must master the intricacies of traditional media to secure favorable coverage and maintain relevance in the public discourse.

- **Beyond Punctuality**: Meeting deadlines transcends mere punctuality; it is a strategic maneuver with profound implications. By consistently meeting deadlines, candidates not only fulfill their obligations but also actively shape the narrative surrounding their campaign, seizing control of the public discourse and shaping perceptions.

- **Seizing Opportunities**: Meeting deadlines allows time for incumbents to prepare a rebuttal to negative narratives and challengers to leverage timely responses to introduce themselves, define their platform, and garner support for their candidacy. In both cases, adherence to deadlines serves as a powerful tool for shaping public perception and ultimately securing victory on Election Day.

The Road to Victory: In the pursuit of electoral victory incumbents and challengers both must recognize the indispensable role of traditional media engagement. By embracing deadlines and strategically engaging with newspapers, radio, and television, candidates position themselves favorably in the eyes of the electorate. In doing so, you maximize your chances of success, ensuring that your message resonates far and wide, ultimately leading to victory at the polls.

Chapter 39

Mastering Impromptu Interviews

Being Ready for Anything

PICTURE THIS SCENARIO: you're thrust in front of a microphone, cameras rolling, and the voters eyes fixed on you.

- What do you say?
- How do you grab their attention and hold it?

The answer lies in crafting a narrative that strikes a chord deep within your audience. It's about understanding their hopes, fears, and dreams, and weaving your platform into a story that speaks directly to their souls.

- **Radiate Confidence and Authenticity**: When you step into the spotlight unprepared, your presence is your greatest asset. Confidence, poise, and authenticity are your armor. Lock eyes with your audience and speak like you're sharing a secret, let your voice resonate with unwavering conviction, and use pauses to punctuate your message. By staying true to yourself and your beliefs, you'll leave a lasting imprint that lingers long after the cameras stop rolling.

- **Navigate the Rough Waters with Grace**: Impromptu interviews are a battleground of challenges - from hard-hitting questions to unexpected twists. But here's the

109

thing: adversity is your ally. This is your chance to shine, proving to the world that you're not just a leader you're a beacon of resilience and strength. Embrace the tough topics, the uncomfortable queries, and show the world what you're made of. Approach each obstacle with grace and clarity, turning potential stumbling blocks into moments of connection and understanding.

• **Forge Meaningful Connections**: At the heart of every impromptu interview lies one crucial element: engagement. Listen to their concerns, address their questions sincerely, and let them know their voices matter. Because when you cultivate genuine connections, you're not just winning votes - you're building a community bound by trust and shared values.

• **Navigating the Terrain**: Seasoned incumbents and bold challengers must master the intricacies of traditional media to secure favorable coverage and maintain relevance in the public discourse!

• **Beyond Punctuality**: When interacting with traditional media consistently and meeting deadlines, candidates not only fulfill their obligations but also actively shape the narrative surrounding their campaign, seizing control of the public discourse and shaping perceptions. This reliability bolsters a candidate's credibility and trustworthiness, qualities indispensable for those defending their position or seeking to carve out a new space in the political arena. Meeting deadlines transcends mere punctuality; it is a strategic manoeuvre with profound implications.

• **Radiate Confidence and Authenticity**: When you step into the spotlight prepared, your presence is your greatest asset. It's not just about the words you utter- it's about how you carry yourself. Confidence, poise, and authenticity are your armor. Lock eyes with your audience like you're sharing a secret, let your voice resonate with unwavering conviction, and use pauses to punctuate your message. By staying true to yourself and your beliefs, you'll leave a lasting imprint that lingers long after the cameras stop rolling.

Chapter 40

Case Study

BARACK OBAMA and Narendra Modi's campaigns demonstrate how a well-rounded media strategy, encompassing traditional and digital platforms, can significantly impact political campaigns and voter engagement.

Barack Obama's 2008 Presidential Campaign: Utilized newspapers to reach traditional voters and add credibility to their messaging; Radio ads and interviews played a crucial role in reaching African American and rural voters; TV ads, including a 30-minute infomercial aired on prime-time television shortly before the election and social media (Facebook, Myspace), email newsletters, and a dedicated campaign website to mobilize younger voters.

Narendra Modi's 2014 Indian General Election Campaign: placed strategic advertisements in newspapers across various states, targeting both urban and rural populations; Radio extensively to reach voters in rural and semi-urban areas; TV advertising and coverage. Major news channels featured his rallies and speeches and Twitter, Facebook, and YouTube to connect with youth and tech-savvy voters.

Part Nine

Winning Political Debates

Chapter 41

Being Equipped and Organized
Preparing for Success

• **PREPARE FOR THE ARENA**: Political debates are battlegrounds where wit, intellect, and preparation collide. Mastery of debate intricacies is a strategic imperative that can shape political careers.

• **Forge Your Arsenal**: Before stepping onto the stage, arm yourself with thorough research and organization.

• **Strike with Clarity:** Speak plainly and concisely to ensure your message reaches every corner of the audience. Organize arguments logically to drive points home with precision.

Chapter 42

Mastering the Art of Persuasion
Influencing with Confidence

Capture Attention: Capturing and holding the audience's attention is half the battle. Engage actively; incorporate storytelling using anecdotes, or humor to leave a lasting impression.

- **Wear Your Confidence**: Confidence is your armor against doubt and skepticism. Project it with unwavering certainty through body language, tone, and demeanor.
- **Adapt and Conquer**: Embrace diversity in thought and opinion to win hearts and minds. Tailor your communication style to suit the audience's preferences.
- **Counter with Grace**: Effective rebuttals demonstrate knowledge and constructive engagement. Anticipate blows and bury them with finesse.

Chapter 43

Seize Victory with Delivery
Captivating Your Audience

• **PRACTICE YOUR DELIVERY:** Practice makes ready, so practice often.

• **Embrace Feedback**: Seek criticism as fuel for growth. Listen, learn, and evolve into the debater you were meant to be.

• **Embody Authenticity**: Speak from the heart and let genuine passion shine through. Embrace your unique voice and perspective to forge genuine connections.

Chapter 44

Case Study

RONALD REAGAN and Barack Obama exemplified different styles of effective debating: Reagan through his use of humor and relatable communication, and Obama through his eloquence and intellectual rigor.

Ronald Reagan: 1980 Presidential Debate against Jimmy Carter

Memorable Moment: Reagan's famous line, "There you go again," effectively deflected Carter's criticism and portrayed Reagan as calm and confident. This phrase became iconic, demonstrating Reagan's ability to use humor and simplicity to disarm his opponent.

Communication Style: Reagan had a unique ability to connect with the audience through clear, concise messaging and a warm demeanor. His background as an actor contributed to his excellent stage presence and delivery.

Barack Obama: 2008 Presidential Debate against John McCain

Memorable Moment: During the debates, Obama consistently displayed a calm and composed demeanor, effectively addressing McCain's criticisms while outlining his policy proposals in a clear and articulate manner. One notable instance was his response to McCain's criticism on foreign policy, where Obama confidently laid out his vision, showing his preparedness and depth of knowledge.

Communication Style: Obama was known for his eloquence and ability to convey complex ideas in an accessible manner. His background as a constitutional law professor contributed to his debating skills, allowing him to argue his points with precision and clarity.

Part Ten

Strategies to Unseat a Political Incumbent

The major factors of political campaigning against an incumbent for a challenger are gaining visibility and difficulties in fundraising. By addressing these dynamics with strategic planning and innovative tactics, a challenger can effectively compete against an incumbent and level the playing field in the campaign process.

Chapter 45

Do the Math

In politics, numbers reign supreme, the calculations tilt in the challenger favor if they are worked methodically and effectively.

- 80% plus of all registered voters <u>don't</u> vote.
- The reaming 16 - 20% registered voting public doesn't hear from the incumbent until the election period.
- A challenger can win if they truly work at winning.

Chapter 46

Planting the Seeds of Change
Laying the Groundwork

THE WINNING COMBINATION;
- A formidable candidate
- A committed and focused campaign team
- Financially supported
- Preparation

Preparation requires meticulous planning and nurturing relationships over time, in this case a minimum of two years. Two years may seem like an eternity, but that time frame [two years] is crucial for cultivating fertile ground building your base where victory begins.

Chapter 47

Pathways to Victory
Navigating the Road to Success

For any of the following strategies and tactics to be effective, all activities stated must take place within the residential voting boundaries of the political seat in question.

PATHWAY ONE: PERSUASION AND INSPIRATION

This pathway focuses on building a strong following within your target voting district to compliment your already built voting bloc.

Persuading Active Voters:

• Target Group:

o Residents who consistently participate in the election process and are looking for or open to new leadership.

o Residents who have recently moved into the voting district and aren't aware of the current political landscape.

o Residents who recently registered to vote and live in the voting district eager to participate and open to change.

• Strategy:

o Develop tailored messages that resonate with the values

and priorities of each specific age and ethnic group within the voting district.

• Goal: Secure 27-31% of all voters within your voting district to compliment your already built voting bloc:

o 7% of residents who consistently participate in the election process and are looking for or open to new leadership.

o 10% of residents who have recently moved into the voting district and aren't aware of the current political landscape.

o 10% of residents who recently registered to vote and live in the voting district eager to participate and open to change.

PATHWAY TWO: SEIZING OPPORTUNITY

The incumbent has reached term limits or decided not to run again. This pathway focuses on building a strong following within your target voting district to compliment your already built voting bloc.

Persuading Active Voters:

• Target Group:

o Residents who consistently participate in the election process and are looking for new leadership.

o Residents who have recently moved into the voting district and aren't aware of the current political landscape.

o Residents who recently registered to vote and live in the voting district eager to participate and open to change.

• Strategy:

o Develop tailored messages that resonate with the values and priorities of each specific age and ethnic group within the voting district.

• Goal: Secure 32% + of all voters within your voting district to compliment your already built voting bloc::

. . .

Pathway Three: Riding the Wave of Discontent

Something has gone wrong and the incumbent has fallen out of favor with the majority of consistent district voters. This pathway focuses on building a strong following within your target voting district to compliment your already built voting bloc.

Persuading Active Voters:

• Target Group:

o Residents who consistently participate in the election process and are looking for or open to new leadership.

o Residents who have recently moved into the voting district and aren't aware of the current political landscape.

o Residents who recently registered to vote and live in the voting district eager to participate and open to change.

• Strategy:

o Develop tailored messages that resonate with the values and priorities of each specific age and ethnic group within the voting district.

• Goal: Secure 27-31% of all voters within your voting district to compliment your already built voting bloc:

o 7% of residents who consistently participate in the election process and are looking for or open to new leadership.

o 10% of residents who have recently moved into the voting district and aren't aware of the current political landscape.

10% of residents who recently registered to vote and live in the voting district eager to participate and open to change.

Chapter 48

Case Study

ALEXANDRIA OCASIO-CORTEZ and Scott Brown These examples illustrate how effectively communicating a resonant message, establishing a personal connection with voters, and maintaining a focused, committed campaign can lead to the unseating of an incumbent or a heavily favored candidate.

Alexandria Ocasio-Cortez (AOC) vs. Joe Crowley (2018)

How She Succeeded:

Effective Communication: AOC utilized a grass-roots campaign with a clear, progressive message that resonated with many voters in her district. She emphasized issues like Medicare for All, tuition-free public college, and criminal justice reform.

Personal Connection: Ocasio-Cortez, a young bartender and activist from the Bronx, connected personally with voters. Her background and story resonated with the everyday experiences of many constituents.

Focused Commitment: Her campaign was highly focused and energetic, leveraging social media effectively and organizing strong on-the-ground efforts. She and her team knocked on thousands of doors and held numerous community events, ensuring her message reached a broad audience.

Targeting Voter Turnout: Understanding the demographics and needs of her district allowed her to mobilize a previously underrepresented base of voters, particularly young and minority communities.

Scott Brown vs. Martha Coakley (2010)
How He Succeeded:
Effective Communication: Brown ran a campaign that focused on being a "different kind of Republican," emphasizing fiscal conservatism, opposition to the Affordable Care Act (Obamacare), and a general populist message that appealed to many Massachusetts voters.

Personal Connection: He portrayed himself as a relatable, everyman candidate, famously driving an old pickup truck around the state as a symbol of his connection to ordinary voters. This image contrasted with Coakley's perceived elitism.

Focused Commitment: Brown's campaign was highly disciplined and proactive. He capitalized on Coakley's missteps and complacency, taking advantage of her limited campaign activities and perceived disconnect from the electorate.

Mobilizing the Base: His campaign successfully energized Republican voters in a traditionally Democratic state, while also appealing to independents and disillusioned Democrats. He leveraged the enthusiasm of the Tea Party movement, which was gaining momentum at the time.

Part Eleven

Crafting a Comprehensive Campaign Battle Plan

Chapter 49

Customization you're Approach

Because no two political landscapes are alike, battle plan customization rules the day. Campaign Managers must tailor an approach to fit the very fabric of the community the candidate seeks to serve.

Chapter 50

Jump Starting Your Campaign

Hitting the Ground Running

MAKE IT HAPPEN: By this point you've been active for a minimum of two years within your voting district establishing your voting base of supporters (Totaling 20% of the previous elections 51% winning number) and now you're ready to start officially campaigning.

• Assemble your campaign team three weeks prior to the official election filing date setting the stage for success.

• Local/City Campaign Races: Start campaigning five months (150 days) before Election Day.

• County Campaign Races: Start campaigning nine months (270 days) before Election Day.

• Statewide Campaign Races: Start campaigning twenty months (600 days) before Election Day.

• National Campaign Races: Start campaigning fifty months (1500 days) before Election Day.

Chapter 51

Create an Action Plan
Mapping Out Your Steps

(WEEKS 1): Like architects drafting blueprints for a skyscraper you've started laying your campaign groundwork. You've hired your campaign manager (CM) and together you identify, contact and hire your campaign core team members.

(Weeks 2 and throughout the campaign process): With your foundation in place turn your attention to securing the resources needed to fuel the campaign journey. Through strategic fundraising initiatives and meticulous financial planning make sure your campaign is financially equipped to compete.

(Weeks 3 and throughout the campaign process): Your team meets regularly to learn, understand and practices how to deliver the campaigns message in a clear and personalized way that speaks directly to the hopes and fears of the residents within your voting districts.

(Weeks 4): With your message honed and campaign platform solidified, from policy rollouts to televised debates, you are prepared and ready to showcase your competence and vision, earning the trust and respect of the voting public.

(Weeks 5 and throughout the campaign process): In a world where perception is reality, through strategic media engagements (social media, podcasts, print, radio, etc.) your campaign advertising message crafted in storytelling format painting a vivid picture of your vision for a better tomorrow for residents needs to start.

(Weeks 6-21): Leveraging the latest data analytics tools your organized grassroots canvassing efforts combined with community meetings and attending neighborhood barbecues, your volunteers become ambassadors of change in your voting district forging personal connections that transcend the digital divide.

(Weeks 7-21): Know where you stand; nightly your team reviews that day's campaign activities, submitting a perceived block by block voter tally, planning strategic moves for the next day's efforts.

(Week-21): Election Day and Post-Election Follow-Up

As the dust settles and the ballots are tallied, your team and you stand on the precipice of history. Celebrating victory is your main thing – winning the election! Nonetheless should the unthinkable occur you must regroup for the next battle; it's about building a better future for generations to come.

Chapter 52

Case Study

BARACK OBAMA'S 2008 Presidential Campaign

Context:

• Demographics: Diverse, with significant young voter base and minority communities.

• Political Climate: Desire for change after two terms of George W. Bush, economic recession, and wars in Iraq and Afghanistan.

Strategies:

Grassroots Mobilization:

• Community Organizing: Leveraged Obama's background as a community organizer to connect with local groups and create a strong network of volunteers.

• Local Offices: Established numerous local offices to ensure strong, on-the-ground presence.

Digital and Social Media Campaigning:

• Innovative Use of Technology: Utilized social media platforms like Facebook and Twitter extensively to engage with younger voters and spread the campaign message.

Data Analytics:

• Employed advanced data analytics to target specific voter segments with tailored messages and mobilize voters effectively.

Message of Hope and Change:

• Inspirational Messaging: Focused on a positive, forward-looking message that resonated with the desire for change and hope, which was a stark contrast to the status quo.

• Inclusive Appeal: Addressed issues pertinent to various demographic groups, ensuring the campaign's message resonated broadly across the electorate.

Narendra Modi's 2014 Indian General Election Campaign

Context:

• Demographics: Vast and diverse electorate, including rural and urban populations, various castes, and religious communities.

• Political Climate: Widespread dissatisfaction with the incumbent Congress party, economic challenges, and corruption scandals.

Strategies:

Development and Governance Focus:

• Economic Development: Promised strong economic growth and development, addressing the common desire for jobs and better infrastructure.

• Governance and Corruption: Emphasized clean governance and efficient administration, appealing to voters tired of corruption.

Localized Campaigning:

• Customized Messaging: Tailored messages to resonate

with local issues and concerns. For example, highlighting water issues in rural areas and job creation in urban areas.

Regional Leaders and Alliances: Partnered with regional leaders and formed strategic alliances to bolster support in specific states and communities.

Extensive Use of Media and Technology:

• Social Media Engagement: Employed social media to reach out to younger and tech-savvy voters, creating a direct line of communication and engagement.

Hologram Rallies: Used innovative technology like 3D hologram rallies to virtually appear in multiple locations simultaneously, maximizing reach and visibility

Epilogue

WELCOME to the pivotal conclusion of *Power Play*, where the intricacies of political strategy have been unveiled, revealing the coveted keys to capturing the hearts and minds of voters. Consider this book as your personal vehicle owner's manual, a navigational guide to understanding and maneuvering through the complex terrain of politics. But remember, possessing knowledge alone does not guarantee victory in the political arena.

Action is the catalyst; it is the decisive and resolute application of acquired knowledge that carves the path to victory. Just as one undergoes driving lessons to master practical skills and cultivate responsible driving habits, so too must political players sharpen their abilities through active engagement and strategic implementation.

As we transition into *Maken IT*, the forthcoming chapter of *Power Play* envisions it as your indispensable companion on this journey - a driving instructor of sorts, adeptly steering you through every twist and turn of the political campaign process. Prepare to navigate with finesse and precision, harnessing the power of informed action to propel your campaign towards success.

Winning an election requires significant time, effort, money, and support. The information outlined in this guide is not a guarantee of victory; they are tools, guidelines, and knowledge. You are the difference maker.

I trust this guidebook will help transform readers and users into political campaign winners and winners into political representatives for positive change.

Thank you for placing your trust in me and these words.

SE Scott

www.ingramcontent.com/pod-product-compliance
Lightning Source LLC
Chambersburg PA
CBHW071329150726

47997CB00002B/657